AF601957

Where the heart finds warmth by a small fire, every corner becomes a treasure, and every morning light feels like home.

~ Caja Frode

Deep in the woods,
in a clearing big,
Where winds blow gently,
and city sounds don’t seep,

Where the forest birds sing,
so soft and mellow,
Lies my little cottage,
with a roof thatched yellow.

Silence whispers,
soft and clear—
No bustling roads,
no noise to hear.

Just rustling leaves
and a deer’s hop,
A peaceful calm
that never stops.

A stone path winds
to a wooden door;
Beside it are pots
with flowers I adore.

The walls are bright
and painted with white,
With windows that let
in plenty of light.

The cottage is small,
smaller than a house,
But I am happy here,
so long's my heart allows.

With a fuzzy rug
and a fireplace bright,
It keeps me warm
through each chilly night.

My cat curls up
in a comfy nook,
While I sit down to read
my favourite book.

The couch is soft,
the quilt hand-sewn—
A cozy space
I call my own.

The kitchen, though small,
is near and dear,
With pots and pans
passed through the years.

From mother's kettle
to grandma's oven,
I make tea and bread,
which I enjoy so often.

By the kitchen window,
my little garden grows,
Full of fruits and flowers
like strawberries and rose.

I plant the seeds
and watch them sprout,
And year after year,
it feeds me throughout.

Outside my home,
the bunnies play,
With twitching noses
and fur so grey.

The colourful birds
sing all day—
Their cheerful songs,
keep my worries away.

The trees around
are lush and green;
The grass is full,
and the air is clean.

The sky above,
so vast and blue,
Fills my eyes
with a beautiful view

The days are simple,
but filled with grace,
With every corner
a special place.

Each morning light,
and each starry night,
Makes my little cottage
feel just right.

Fin

www.ingramcontent.com/pod-product-compliance
Ingram Content Group UK Ltd.
Pitfield, Milton Keynes, MK11 3LW, UK
UKHW060110300726
14090UKWH00002B/115

* 9 7 8 9 9 1 4 7 6 8 9 3 0 *